Composition through Pictures

Other Books by J. B. Heaton

Fables from the Far East
Stories from Ancient China (*with Michael West*)
Selected Tests in Reading
Overseas Students' Companion to English (*with J. P. Stocks*)
Graded English Test Papers (*with J. P. Stocks*)
Prepositions and Adverbial Particles
Using Prepositions and Particles Workbooks One, Two and Three
Stories from Shakespeare (*with Michael West*)
The Stone Mother & Child
Remove English (*with J. Hobbs*)
Effective Comprehension (*with K. Methold*)
English Examination Practice (*with J. P. Stocks & R. Hawkey*)

Composition through Pictures
J. B. Heaton

Illustrations by James Moss

Longman

Pearson Education Limited
Edinburgh Gate, Harlow
Essex CM20 2JE, England
and Associated Companies throughout the world.

www.longman.com

© J. B. Heaton 1966

All rights reserved; no part of this publication may be
reproduced, stored in a retrieval system, or transmitted
in any form or by any means, electronic, mechanical,
photocopying, recording, or otherwise, without
the prior written permission of the Copyright owner.

*First published *1966*
*New impressions * 1967 (thrice); * 1968;*
** 1969; * 1971 (twice); * 1972;*
** 1973 (twice); * 1974; * 1975;*
** 1976; * 1977; * 1978; * 1979;*
** 1980; * 1981; * 1983; * 1984;*
** 1985 (twice); * 1986 (twice); * 1987;*
** 1988 (thrice); *1989; *1990 (twice); *1992; *1993; *1994; *1995*
   Eighty-third impression 2004

Printed in Malaysia, PA

ISBN 0-582-52125-4

Contents

Picture Composition	Subject	No. of Pictures	Page
1	Description	1	1
2	Story	3	2
3	Instructions	6	3 & 4
4	Description	1	5
5	Story	3	6
6	Instructions	6	7 & 8
7	Description	1	9
8	Comparison	2	10
9	Story	3	11
10	Directions (Map)	1	12
11	Instructions	6	13 & 14
12	Description	1	15
13	Comparison	2	16
14	Story	3	17
15	Directions (Map)	1	18
16	Instructions	6	19 & 20
17	Story	6	21 & 22
18	Story	6	23 & 24
19	Story	6	25 & 26
20	Story	6	27 & 28
21	Story	6	29 & 30
22	Story	6	31 & 32
23	Story	6	33 & 34
24	Story	6	35 & 36
25	Story	6	37 & 38
26	Story	6	39 & 40
27	Story	6	41 & 42
28	Story	6	43 & 44
29	Story	6	45 & 46
30	Story	6	47 & 48
31	Story	6	49 & 50
32	Story	6	51 & 52
Appendix: (1)	List of Sentence Patterns		54
(2)	Helpful Phrases		54

Foreword to the Teacher

The use of pictures for oral and written composition has many advantages which have not yet been fully explored in the teaching of English as a second language. In addition to developing the pupil's powers of observation, picture composition encourages clear and precise thinking while helping the pupil to talk and write freely upon a definite subject. Pictures are of great help in the teaching of new vocabulary and structures, and provide the pupil with the basic material for his composition, thus enabling him to give his full attention to the correct use of language. At the same time, his imaginative powers are stimulated by means of the pictures.

The pictures for composition have been carefully selected so that the basic vocabulary required for each composition is controlled. However, as each picture composition is built up around one particular theme or topic, new words not included in the pupil's active vocabulary are sometimes required. All such words are both illustrated in the pictures and listed below the pictures. Key words or difficult words are also included in the lists. Sometimes the same word is useful for different compositions and may appear more than once in the vocabulary lists.

Also given for each composition is one sentence pattern, on which the pupil can concentrate. In certain cases, two sentence patterns are given. Each sentence pattern appears in the form of a substitution table and should be thoroughly practised before the pupil begins the composition. Opportunity is provided usually in Exercise 3 for the sentence pattern to be used at least once, and the pupil should be strongly encouraged to use the sentence pattern in his composition work. Note that the sentence patterns are written in the Present tense in Picture Compositions 1—24; the Past tense is used in the sentence patterns for Picture Compositions 25 to 32. Note also that not all the sentences in the substitution tables relate to the picture(s) : other sentences have been added in the tables in order to give sufficient practice in the use of the pattern.

The aim of introducing important words and structures is to give the pupil a thorough preparation for the composition work. The importance of a thorough preparation for both oral and written composition cannot be too greatly stressed at this stage. Generally, the teacher is advised to complete the oral preparation and questions before beginning any written work (although this rule is not, of course, an inflexible one).

Each composition may be treated as primarily oral or as primarily written. Preparatory exercises may be organised in a number of different ways. If he considers that the class requires additional preparation, the teacher may care to introduce the Look and Point method. For example, *before* asking the ten questions about Picture Composition 1, he may ask the children to look and point to the three children playing with a ball, the man who is reading, etc. Alternatively, *after* asking questions about Picture Composition 17, he may wish to read out six sentences, each describing one of the pictures in the story. Thus, he may say : 'The ball floats on the water' or 'The boy kicks the ball high into the air', etc. and he will ask the class to look at and point to the appropriate picture.

Written work can be set either as further preparation for composition writing or else as follow-up work. Here are some examples of just a few of the different types of written exercises which may be set :—

1. Vocabulary. (Picture Composition 1) Choose the correct word from the brackets : Two people are (jumping, swimming, falling, diving) off the raft.

2. Prepositions and adverbs. (Picture Composition 15) You are telling someone how to go from Seaview Gardens to the cinema. Complete these directions by filling in the blanks : 'Go _____ North Street _____ Hill Street. Then turn _____ ....'

3. Verbs : tenses. (Picture Composition 11) Put the verbs into the correct form. Make any changes which are necessary. 'After (hang) the pan from the long stick, (light) the fire. (Sit) down and (wait) until the water (boil) before (take) the stick away ....'

4. Verbs : forms. (Picture Composition 20) Rewrite these sentences, using the correct form of the verb in brackets. Two boys are going (to fish, fishing). The captain of the ship enjoyed (to listen, listening) to the boys.

5. Articles. (Picture Composition 10) Fill in the blanks with *a*, *an*, or *the* only where necessary : There is a bridge over_____ River Whiting.

6 Sentence Construction. (Picture Composition 21) Join the correct parts and write out the complete sentences. (Each part should be used once only.)

The little boy	that the little boy cannot read.
The rich man	comes through the small hole.
It is so dark	is very poor.
A hammer and a chisel	for the little boy to study.
The light	lives in the big house.
Now there is enough light	are very useful tools.

Other exercises may be introduced to bring in imaginary conversations between the people in a picture. The pupil may also be given simple comprehension questions on the contents of a picture. Although the teacher may make unlimited use of the pictures for language work, he should never lose sight of the fact that each picture or series of pictures is designed chiefly for one purpose—the teaching of composition. Exercises are generally useful only to the extent that they are directly related to the composition work. The first half of the book contains pictures for description, pictures for comparison, pictures which tell short stories, and maps and pictures for simple instructions. The second half contains pictures which tell slightly longer stories. The appendix contains a list of the chief structures and also helpful phrases for describing the pictures. Some teachers may prefer their pupils not to use this section at all. The sentence patterns relating to the last eight stories in the book contain the past tense. All the questions in Exercise 3 of each picture composition, however, are framed in the present to convey a greater sense of immediacy and participation. Throughout the book, Exercise 4 may be given as an oral composition or as a written composition. Pupils must be encouraged and helped to make the characters in each story real and alive : for this reason particularly, they should be instructed to give a name to each character. The naming of characters is an important step towards composition for visualisation and identification.

The pupil should spend a few minutes looking at each picture or set of pictures before the teacher asks questions about them. He should be told to listen very carefully to the teacher and to watch the teacher's lips as he asks each question. It is hoped that he will find the compositions varied and interesting.

1

1 beach, spade, sun-glasses, camera, life-guard, raft ; asleep, crowded ; throw, cover, make a film, drown, rescue, dive, swim.

2

They are running towards We are watching Richard is looking at	a girl a fat man	who	is asleep. cannot swim. is reading a book.

3

a What is the boy with the spade doing ?
b Where is the ball falling ?
c What is the fat man doing ?
d What are the two men using ?
e What are they doing ?
f Where is the big man running ?
g What is the girl in the water doing ?
h Where are the three swimmers going ?
i Are there many people on the raft ?
j How many people can you see on the beach ?

4 Describe this picture.

2

1 sports-car, driver, pedestrian, umbrella, pool, zebra-crossing, kerb, cyclist, passenger ; splash.

2

The driver is splashing the people		going near them.
He makes the policeman angry	by	being careless.
Jim may cause an accident		hurrying in the rain.
You will not pass the driving-test		driving so quickly.

3
a What is in front of the car in Picture 1 ?
b Why are the people carrying umbrellas ?
c How is the driver splashing the people ?
d What is the woman in front of the car waiting to do ?
e What is the car passing in Picture 2 ?
f Why is the driver laughing ?
g Where is the car in Picture 3 ?
h Where is the bus ?
i Why is the driver angry ?
j What are the people in the bus doing ?

4 Tell this story.

3

1

2

3

1 shape, model, aeroplane, cardboard, paint-box, fuselage, wing, tail, slot, scissors, knife, directions ; dotted (line) ; cut out, fold, glue.

2

Use	a knife this tool some scissors	to cut	the cardboard. the model aeroplane. the thick string.

3
a What is the boy painting in Picture 1 ?
b What is he using to cut out the shape of the aeroplane in Picture 2 ?
c What directions can you see near the dotted line in the aeroplane ?
d What is the boy using the knife to do in Picture 3 ?
e What can you see on the table near the bottom of the picture ?
f What has the boy just done in Picture 4 ?
g Where is the brush ?
h What is the boy cutting in Picture 5 ?
i Where is he putting the wings in Picture 6 ?
j Why do you think he is smiling happily in this picture.?

4 Tell someone how to make a model aeroplane.

1 sitting-room, arm-chair, sofa, newspaper, cabinet, television (set), radio (set), thief, mask, knit; steal, notice; comfortably, silently.

2

I The people in the room We John and Peter	do not know	what is happening. who is there. where the thieves are. when the visitors came.

3
a Are the two children watching television?
b Where are they?
c Who is sitting in the arm-chair?
d What is the old woman doing?
e Where is the dog?
f Is the cabinet in front of the sofa?
g What are the two men wearing over their faces?
h What is one man carrying?
i What is the other man doing?
j Do the people in the room know what is happening?

4 Describe this picture.

5

1 bank (of a river), fisherman, fishing-line, swimmer, bather, hook, boot, surface, (a) catch; surprised; bathe; under water (swim under water).

2

He is My mother is The children are	surprised pleased	to	see the boot. meet Mrs Lee. find out about the test. hear about your adventure.

3

a What is the old man doing?
b Where are the two small children standing?
c What are the boys doing under the bridge?
d Where is one of the boys swimming?
e Why cannot the old man see the boy in Picture 2?
f Where is the boot?
g What is the boy doing?
h What is the old man surprised to see in Picture 3?
i What are the two children doing?
j Where is the boy swimming now?

4 Tell this story.

6

1 2 3

1 kitchen, kettle, tap, sink, shelf, stove, gas, steam, teapot, teacup, tea-spoon, milk-jug, sugar basin, saucer; boil, pour.

2

When	the cup is clean, the water is boiling, the tea is ready, the milk is finished,	please tell me. bring it to us.

3
a Where is the girl in Picture 1?
b What is she doing?
c Where is she putting the kettle in Picture 2?
d How can you tell in Picture 3 that the water is boiling?
e How much water is the girl pouring into the teapot in this picture?
f What is she doing in Picture 4?
g What is happening in Picture 5?
h Where is the girl pouring the water in Picture 6?
i What else is on the table?
j What has she just done in the six pictures?

4 Tell someone how to make a cup of tea.

7

1 camp, camp-fire, camp-site, valley, tent, (the) washing, fence, bull, farmer, clothes-line, bicycle; chase, shake, disappear; angrily.

2

| We must hurry
Mary is crying
The boys are running | because | the farmer is angry.
it is raining.
there is a bull. |

3
a Where are the boys camping?
b How many tents are there?
c Where is the clothes-line?
d What is the boy up the tree doing?
e What are the three boys near the fire doing?
f Why are the two boys running out of the field?
g What is one boy climbing over?
h Why is the farmer angry?
i Where are the three bicylces?
j Why does the teacher standing near the bicycles look unhappy?

4 Describe this picture.

8

1 fishing-boat, rowing-boat, yacht, motor-boat, aeroplane, shore, jetty, building, warehouse, wharf, mountain; surround, unload, anchor.

2

I can see There are	more	buildings big ships aeroplanes	here in Picture A in this scene	than	over there. in Picture B. in the other scene.

I can see There are	fewer	buildings big ships aeroplanes	over there in Picture B in the other scene	than	here. in Picture A. in this scene.

3

a What can you see behind the motor-boat in Picture A?
b How many big ships are there in Picture A?
c Where are the aeroplanes in Picture A?
d What can you see behind the ships in Picture A?
e What is behind the motor-boat in Picture B?
f Where is the motor-boat going in Picture B?
g Who are in the rowing-boat?
h What is near the fishing-boats in Picture B?
i Which picture has some yachts in it?
j Are there more buildings in Picture A than in Picture B?

4

a Describe Picture A (orally).
b Write a description of Picture B.
c Compare Picture A with Picture B.

9

1 starter, starting-line, running-track, running-shoes, shorts, competitor, runner, stadium, spectator ; startled ; get ready, run a race, fire a gun, start a race, cheer a person on.

2

They are waiting for	you Mr Brown their friend us	to	start the race. fire the gun. answer the question. run in the race.

3

a How many runners are there in Picture 1 ?
b Where are they ?
c What are they doing ?
d What is the man on the right holding ?
e Where are the spectators ?
f What has the starter just done in Picture 2 ?
g What are the spectators doing ?
h Why is the man startled in Picture 3 ?
i What has he done ?
j Where is the gun ?

4 Tell this story.

10

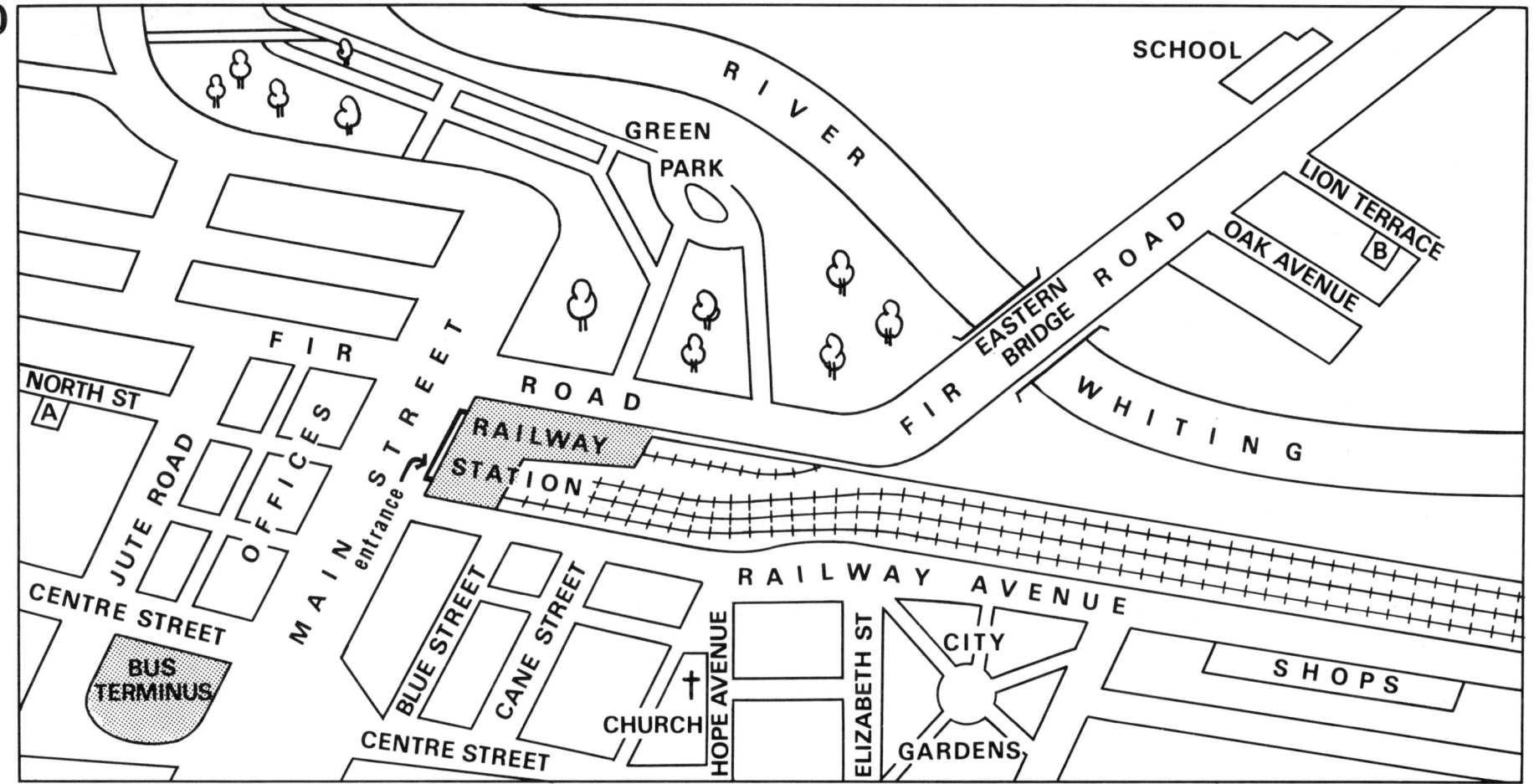

1 gardens, railway station, (bus) terminus ; continue ; opposite, on my left, on my right.

2

	until	
Walk along the road Stay on the bus Don't get off the train Continue on your way	until	you come to Main Street. you reach the terminus. you arrive at Victoria. you see the policeman.

3

a Does A live in North Street?
b Is the church in Blue Street?
c Where does B live?
d Is Green Park near the railway station or the bus terminus?
e What is the bridge called?
f What river does it cross?
g Where are the shops?
h Where is the entrance to the Railway Station?
i If you walked along Hope Avenue towards Railway Avenue, what would you see?
j I want to go to Centre Street from the school. Should I stay on the bus until I reach the terminus?

4 Direct someone from B's house to the shops along Railway Avenue.

11

1 square, twig, fork, tent, handle, camp-fire, sharp, stout, forked; kneel (down), look for, set fire to; firmly.

2

After	cutting the grass, putting the twig in the ground, hanging a pan on the stick, helping Tom,	collect some wood. wait for me. take a rest. light a match.

3

a What is the boy doing in Picture 1?
b What are the other boys doing?
c What can you see behind them?
d What is the boy putting in the centre of the square?
e Where is he putting the other twigs?
f Where is he putting the forked twig in Picture 4?
g What is he holding in Picture 5?
h Where is the pan in Picture 6?
i What is the boy doing now?
j What has he done in the other five pictures?

4 Tell someone how to make a camp-fire.

12

1 crossroads, pavement, traffic, traffic-lights, traffic-jam, driver, policeman, queue, tyre, puncture ; blocked ; hurry, direct (traffic), blow (their) horns.

2

The policeman Mr Green	is telling him is asking me is ordering us	to	stop. go away. push the car.
The policeman Mr Green	is telling him is asking me is ordering us	not to	stop. go away. push the car.

3

a Why has the car in the middle of the road stopped ?
b What is the driver trying to do ?
c What are the other drivers doing ?
d What is the policeman telling the motorist ?
e What is the other policeman trying to do ?
f Where are all the cars ?
g Why can they not move ?
h What kind of buildings are on both sides of the road ?
i What is the boy on the pavement carrying ?
j Why are the people getting off the bus ?

4 Describe this picture.

13

1 stall, counter, bunch of grapes, shopkeeper, cakes, sweets, shelf, packet, flour; displayed, on display, labelled; pick up, bargain.

2

| There are
I can see | as many | people here
eggs in this shop | as | over there.
in the other shop. |

| There are
not
I cannot see | so many | tins of food
packets | in Picture A
here | as | in Picture B.
over there. |

3
a In which picture can you see some fruit?
b How many different kinds of fruit are there? What are they?
c Where are the two boxes of eggs in Picture A?
d What is the girl doing in this picture?
e Who is picking up an apple?
f At whom is the shopkeeper looking in Picture B?
g Are there as many tins of food in Picture A as in Picture B?
h What are the two old women doing in Picture B?
i What can you see inside the glass in the shop?
j If you wanted to buy some flour, would you go to the stall in Picture A or to the shop in Picture B?

4
a Describe Picture A (orally).
b Write a description of Picture B.
c Compare Picture A with Picture B

14

1 hunter, footprint, track, jungle, clearing ; frightened ; (to) track, crouch.

2

	that	
The two hunters are running away so quickly		they drop their gun.
They are looking so closely at the ground		they do not see the tiger.

3
a Where are the two hunters ?
b What are they following ?
c What animals are watching them in Picture 1 ?
d What is watching them in Picture 2 ?
e Why do the two men not see the tiger ?
f What are the two hunters doing in Picture 3 ?
g What has one of them dropped ?
h What is the tiger doing ?
i Where are the monkeys ?
j Why are the two hunters running away ?

4 Tell this story

15

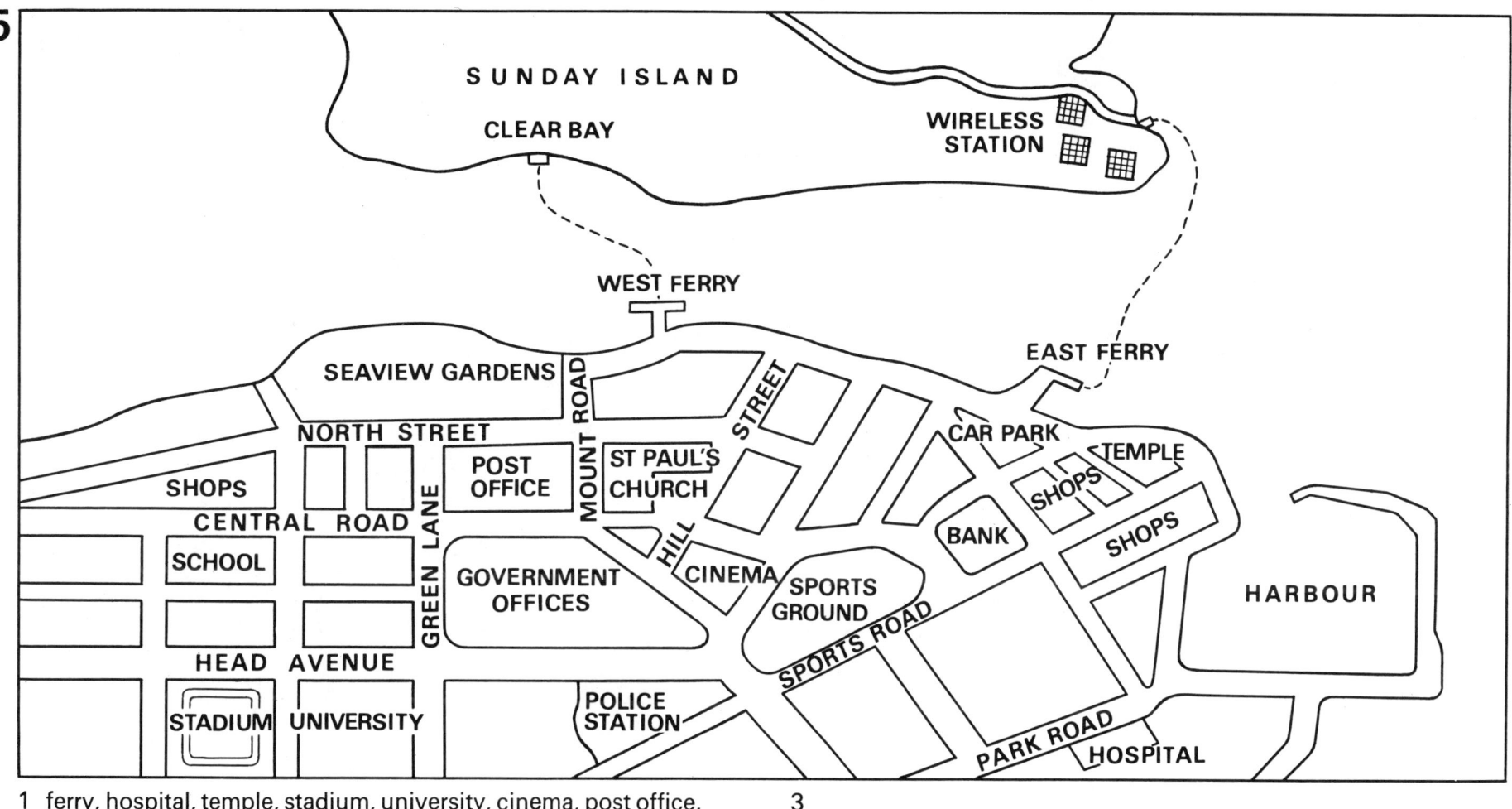

1 ferry, hospital, temple, stadium, university, cinema, post office, wireless station, police station, government offices, sports ground, harbour.

2

Can you please	tell me show us	how to	go to the Post Office? reach the university? find your house? get to the hospital?
Can you please	direct me take us drive Mr Lee	to	the police station? Peter's house? St. Paul's Church? the ferry?

3

a In which road is the hospital?
b What building is next to the stadium?
c Where is the wireless station?
d What road is between St. Paul's Church and the Post Office?
e Which ferry would you catch to Clear Bay?
f What buildings could you see from the Sports Ground?
g Which road would you walk along from the school to the Post Office?
h Ask someone how you can go to the East Ferry.
i Where could you play football?
j What roads run on each side of the Police Station?

4 Direct someone from the university to the temple near the harbour. Mention some of the buildings that he would pass. Describe them in such a way as to help him.

16

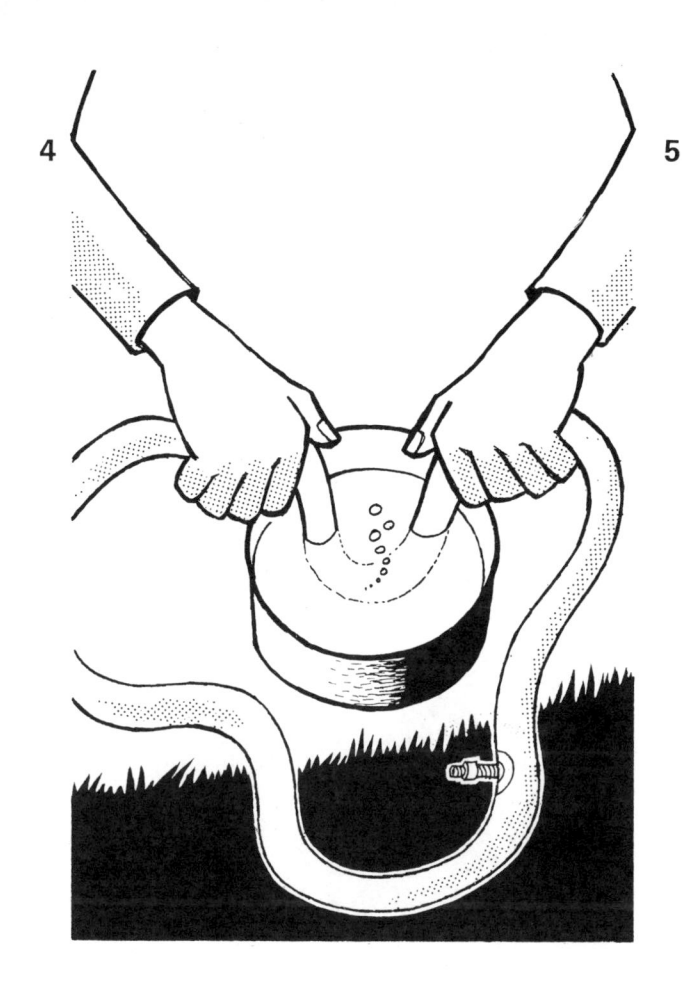

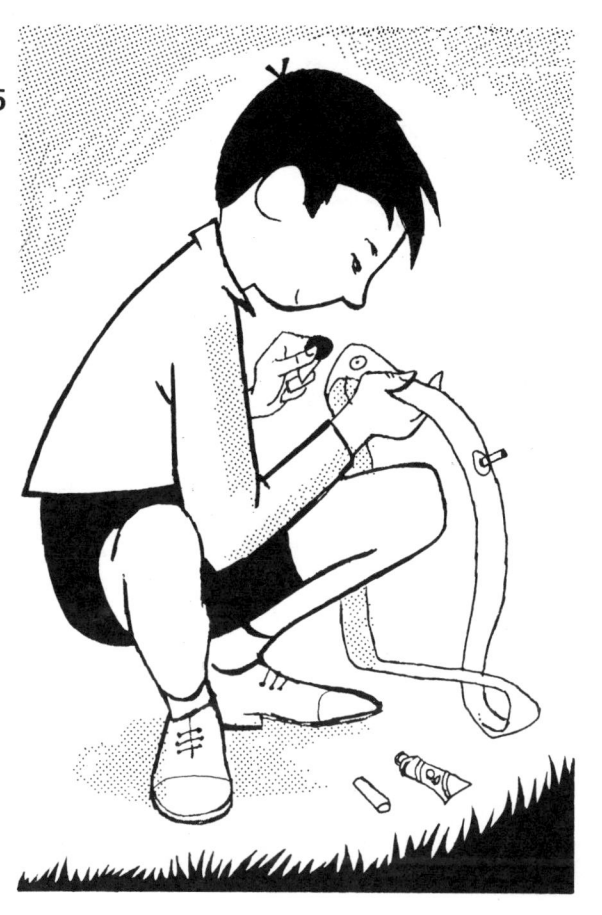

1 rice field, tyre, puncture, (tyre) lever, inner tube, tool kit, pump, saddle-bag, bubble, patch ; flat (tyre) ; cycle, examine, (to) pump (up), (to) mark, stick ; upside down.

2

Before	putting the tube into water, setting off again,	pump it up. look at the tyre.
Mark the spot Make sure that everything is clean	before	sticking the patch on. leaving the camp.

3

a Where is the cyclist in Picture 1 ?
b What has just happened to the tyre of the bicycle ?
c What has the boy done to the bicycle in Picture 2 ?
d What has he just done to the wheel ?
e What is he doing with the tyre levers ?
f Why is the tube no longer flat in Picture 3 ?
g What is the boy doing in this picture ?
h Where are the bubbles coming from ?
i On which part of the tube is the boy sticking the patch ?
j What is the boy doing in Picture 6 ?

4 Tell someone how to mend a puncture.

17

1

2

3

21

1 trunk, hole, butterfly, snake, bowl ; surprised ; kick, catch, miss, roll, kneel, scratch, float.

2

Although	a boy is trying to catch the ball,	he cannot reach it.
	he is feeling for the ball,	it is too far away.
	he can see the kite,	he is too small to get it.

3
a What are the boys doing in Picture 1?
b Where is the ball falling in Picture 2?
c Where is the hole?
d Why is the big boy in Picture 2 running?
e Can the big boy reach the ball in Picture 3?
f Why are the boys in Picture 4 scratching their heads?
g What is the small boy in the distance doing in Picture 4?
h What is he bringing to the hole in Picture 5?
i What is the small boy doing in Picture 6?
j Why are all the boys happy?

4 Tell this story.

18

1

2

3

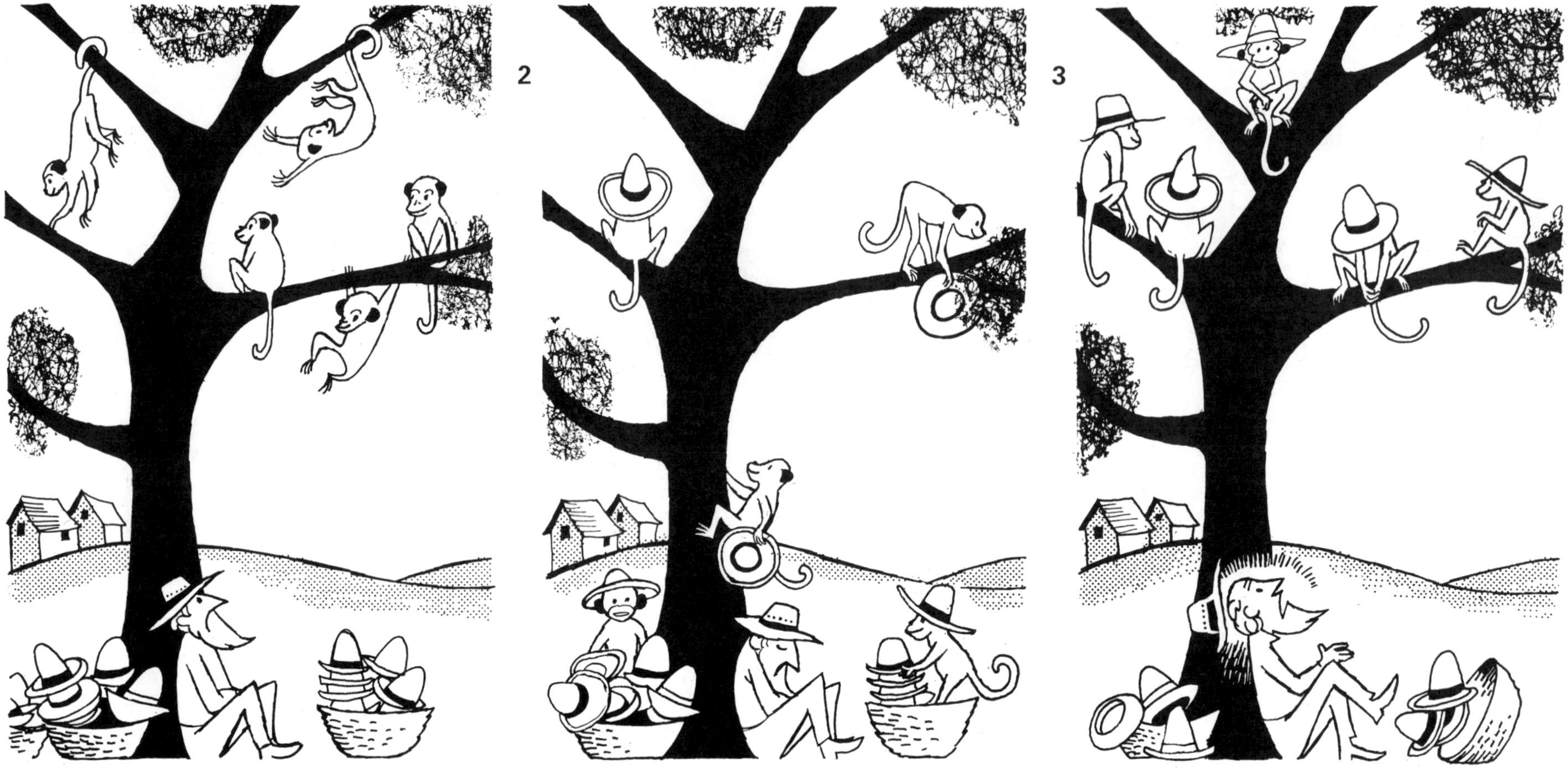

1 beard, monkey, basket, branch, fist, ground ; tired, shocked ;
  fall asleep, wear, awaken, shake, scratch, imitate, pick up.

2

While	the old man is sleeping, he is shouting at them,	the monkeys take the hats. they shake their fists.

The monkeys take the hats They shake their fists	while	the old man is sleeping. he is shouting at them.

3
a Why is the old man sitting down under the tree?
b Where are the monkeys in Picture 1?
c When do the monkeys take the hats in Picture 2?
d What does the old man see when he awakens?
e Why is he shaking his fist at them in Picture 4?
f What are the monkeys doing in this picture?
g Why is the old man scratching his head in Picture 5?
h What are the monkeys doing in this picture?
i Why has the old man thrown his hat on the ground in Picture 6?
j What will the old man do when all the hats are on the ground?

4 Tell this story.

24

19

1 park, lawn, gardener, shoulder, basket, flower-bed;
   strong (wind); kick, sweep, blow, scatter.

2

| The gardener
We
Tony and Mary | must
should
ought to | sweep up all the leaves.
make the lawn tidy.
put them in the basket. |

3
a What does the sign say in Picture 1?
b What can you see on the lawn?
c What must the gardener do?
d What is the gardener doing in Picture 2?
e Where is the basket in Picture 3?
f Where is the gardener putting the leaves?
g What is he doing in the next picture?
h Why is the boy holding his cap on his head?
i What has happened to the leaves in Picture 5?
j Where are the leaves in Picture 6?

4 Tell this story.

20

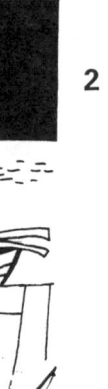

1

2

3

1 fishing-rod, rowing-boat, shore, storm, pan, fishing-boat, skipper, rope, pullover, clothes, deck, (a) present; on board; go fishing, catch fish, (to) notice, sink, wear, admire.

2

They do not	notice see hear	a storm beginning. the wind blowing the trees. the sea becoming rough.
Dick is They are I am	ready to	dive into the sea. throw a rope. help the boys.

3
a What are the three boys carrying in Picture 1?
b Where are the two boys in Picture 2?
c What do they not notice?
d Is the sea calm or rough in Picture 3?
e What is the boy with the pan doing?
f What is the other boy ready to do?
g What is happening to the rowing-boat in Picture 4?
h What is the man on the fishing-boat doing with the rope?
i What are the two boys wearing in Picture 5?
j Where have they got the big fish in Picture 6?

4 Tell this story.

21

1 darkness, jug, neighbour, hammer, chisel ; wealthy ;
say goodbye, peer, decide, send away, shine.

2

| The boy is asking | the rich man | if | he can study in the big house. |
| They are asking | their neighbour | | they can have a lamp. |

| The boy is asking | the rich man | to | let him study in the big house. |
| They are asking | their neighbour | | let them have a lamp. |

3
a Who lives in the small house at the side of the big house?
b Who lives in the big house?
c What is the rich man doing in Picture 1?
d What is the little boy doing in Picture 2?
e Why is he looking very closely at the book?
f What do you think the little boy is asking the rich man in Picture 3?
g What is the rich man telling the little boy?
h Where is the little boy going in Picture 4?
i What is he doing in Picture 5?
j Where is the light coming from?

4 Tell this story.

30

22

1 (play) hide-and-seek, statue, branch, pot, stone; huge; look for, hide, climb, slip, shout, rush, break, tumble out.

2

| The children do not know
Mrs Lee does not know
We already know | what | to do.
to say.
to tell the teacher. |

3
a Where are the children playing?
b What is the big boy doing in Picture 1?
c What are the others doing in this picture?
d What is the small boy doing in Picture 2?
e What is there under the branches of the tree?
f What is happening to him in Picture 3?
g Do the other children know what to do in Picture 4?
h What are the two boys carrying in Picture 5?
i What are these two boys doing in Picture 6?
j How has the small boy got out of the pot in Picture 7?

4 Tell this story.

23

1 **2** **3**

PARP PARP
HONK HONK

1 cyclist, motorist, hedge, bonnet, engine; narrow, (un)hurt;
  blow (his) horn, knock (him) off, set off, break down,
  ring (his) bell; straight on.

2

The road is The streets are This lane is	too	narrow rough dangerous	for	the car to pass. the bus to go quickly. him to drive fast.

3
a What is the boy riding?
b What is the driver of the car doing?
c Why cannot the motorist pass the boy?
d What is he doing in Picture 2?
e What has happened to the boy in Picture 3?
f What is the boy doing in Picture 4?
g What does the boy see in front of him in Picture 5?
h What is the man doing in this picture?
i What has happened to the engine?
j What is the boy doing in Picture 6?

4 Tell this story.

24

1   2   3

35

1 scale, weight, elephant, building, crane, mark, height
pole, shoulder, basket, stone ; (im)possible, exact ; weigh,
find out, lead, sink, kneel, congratulate.

2

It is	possible impossible necessary difficult	to	weigh the baskets of stones. weigh the elephant. put the stones in the boat. mark the side of the boat.

3
a What can you see in the background of Picture 1 ?
b What is the man near the elephant trying to do ?
c Where is the boy taking the elephant in Picture 2 ?
d Where is the elephant in Picture 3 ?
e What is the boy doing in this picture ?
f What are the two men carrying in Picture 4 ?
g What is the man doing with the elephant ?
h What is the boy looking at in Picture 5 ?
i What are the two men doing in Picture 6 ?
j Was it possible to weigh the elephant ?

4 Tell this story.

25

1 kitchen, picnic, picnic-basket, tea-pot, flask, sandwich, map, gate, shade ; startled, surprised, disappointed ; get ready, pour, wave goodbye, jump out, eat up.

2

David and Ann did not eat the food	that	Mrs Brown made.
They took the tea		their mother gave them.
I liked the cake		was in the basket.

3
a What is the small girl doing in the first picture ?
b Where is the boy putting the sandwiches ?
c What is their mother making ?
d What is the dog doing in Picture 2 ?
e Why cannot the two children see the dog ?
f What are the two children doing in Picture 3 ?
g Where are they going in the next picture ?
h What is the little girl doing in Picture 4 ?
i Where is the dog ?
j Why do the two children look surprised in Picture 6 ?

4 Tell this story.

26

TO THE MARKET →

1 merchant, son, donkey, sign, market, fist, bamboo, pole, bridge ; surprised ; lead, scratch, shake, pick up, tie, approach, slide (off) ; angrily, pitifully, sympathetically.

2

The merchant pleased no one He made people angry	because	he tried to please everyone. he put his son on the donkey. he rode on the donkey. he carried the donkey.

3
a Where are the merchant and his son taking the donkey ?
b Why are the people laughing and pointing in Picture 1 ?
c Where is the young boy in Picture 2 ?
d Why is the old man shaking his fist at the young boy ?
e Where is the merchant in Picture 3 ?
f Why does the merchant make the woman and the girl angry ?
g What is the merchant doing in Picture 4 ?
h Where have the merchant and his son put the donkey in Picture 5 ?
i What has happened to the donkey in Picture 6 ?
j Why did the merchant please no one ?

4 Tell this story.

27

1 starting-line, cross-country race, runner, whistle, flag, spectator, hedge, track, shade, finishing-line ; boastful, confident, shady ; boast, approach, decide, take a rest, fall asleep, awake, catch up with ; ahead, in front (of).

2

He was so far in front It was so hot He ran so quickly	that	he wanted to take a rest. he decided to sit down. he began to feel tired.

3
a What are the boys getting ready to do ?
b What is one of the two men holding ?
c Where is the big boy in Picture 2 ?
d What are the two runners behind him doing ?
e What is the big boy doing in Picture 3 ?
f Why does he decide to take a rest ?
g What is the big boy doing in Picture 4 ?
h What is he doing in Picture 5 ?
i Where is the small boy with the number 2 on his shirt in Picture 6 ?
j Why is the big boy angry ?

4 Tell this story.

28

1 helicopter, coins, money, lamp-post, beggar, pity ; blind, poorly-dressed, mistaken, disappointed ; gaze, catch sight of, feel sorry for, bang, drop, (to) thank.

2

The blind man thought	that	the rich woman had given him the money.
Mr and Mrs Robinson knew		the boy had dropped the coins in his tin.
She said		Richard had bought a toy helicopter.

3
a What is the little boy looking at in Picture 1 ?
b Why is he counting his money ?
c Whom does he catch sight of in Picture 2 ?
d What is the man doing ?
e What does the boy feel in Picture 3 ?
f Where is the boy going in the next picture ?
g What is the rich woman doing ?
h What is the boy doing in Picture 5 ?
i How does the blind man know that someone has put some money in his tin ?
j Why is the blind man thanking the rich woman ?

4 Tell this story.

29

1 hockey, hockey-stick, player, goal, river, fisherman, bank, campfire; play (hockey), hit, strike, stare, gather (round), (to) cook.

2

| The two boys ran to the river | so as to | look for their ball. |
| They stopped the game | | take a rest. |

| The two boys ran to the river | so that | they could look for their ball. |
| They stopped the game | | they could take a rest. |

3
a What game are the boys playing?
b What can you see in the background of Picture 1?
c Where has one of the boys hit the ball in Picture 2?
d What is the man doing in this picture?
e Why are some of the boys running to the river?
f Where is the ball in Picture 3?
g What can you see near the ball?
h What are the boys trying to do in Picture 4?
i Why are they laughing in the next picture?
j What are they doing in Picture 6?

4 Tell this story.

46

30

1 transistor radio, tape-recorder, counter, customer, shopkeeper, shelf, show-case, (suit-)case, switch, music, policeman; cunning; (to) display, examine, steal, turn on, switch on, realise, become aware of; accidentally.

2

The thief turned I switched Joan put	on off	the small radio. the television. the light. all the fans.

The thief turned I switched Joan put	the small radio the television the light all the fans	on. off.

3

a Whom can you see in the shop?
b What is the man pointing at in Picture 2?
c What is the shopkeeper doing in Picture 3?
d What is the customer about to do in this picture?
e Where has he put his small case?
f What is he doing in Picture 4?
g What has he accidentally done?
h Where is the radio in Picture 5?
i Why is the shopkeeper pointing at the man and running towards him?
j What has happened to the man in Picture 6?

4 Tell this story.

31

1 inn, innkeeper, staff, scenery, horror, hunter, admiration ; fierce ; persuade, prevent, catch sight of, (to) spring raise, break in two, grasp, strike.

2

He hit the tiger He struck its head Harry was running away Mr Brown was working	as hard as	he could. possible.
The inn keeper tried to We could not He almost managed to	stop him prevent them	from	going. climbing the mountain. leaving home.

3

a What can you see in the picture on the inn wall ?
b What is the innkeeper trying to do ?
c What is the young man doing in Picture 2 ?
d What is there on the right side of the young man ?
e Where is the young man in Picture 3 ?
f What is he looking at ?
g What has happened to the young man's staff in Picture 4 ?
h What has the tiger done in this Picture ?
i What is he doing with his right hand ?
j What are the three men doing in Picture 6 ?

4 Tell this story.

32

1 book-shop, shopkeeper, counter, bookcase, candle, flame, jacket, bravery ; scornful, frightened, pay for, bark, wonder, grow dark, catch fire, blaze, stamp (out), (to) praise.

2

The boy The small child	whom	he left the dog frightened everyone praised we saw here	put out the fire. stayed in the room.
The boy The small child	whose	books were burning jacket was on the floor candle was blown over brother ran away	put out the fire. stayed in the room.

3
a What is the small boy buying in Picture 1 ?
b Where are the two boys in Picture 2 ?
c Why is the big boy laughing at the small boy ?
d Where are the two boys in Picture 3 ?
e Where is the candle in this picture ?
f What is the small boy doing ?
g What has caused the fire in Picture 4 ?
h Why is the big boy running away ?
i What is the small boy doing in Picture 5 ?
j Who put out the fire ?

4 Tell this story.

Appendix

1 List of Sentence Patterns

1. They are running towards | a girl | who | is asleep.
2. The driver is splashing the people | by | going near them.
3. Use | a knife | to cut | the cardboard.
4. I | do not know | what is happening.
5. He is | surprised | to | see the boot.
6. When | the cup is clean, | please tell me.
7. We must hurry | because | the farmer is angry.
8. I can see | more | buildings | here | than | over there.
   I can see | fewer | buildings | over there | than | here.
9. They are waiting for | you | to | start the race.
10. Walk along the road | until | you come to First Street.
11. After | cutting the grass, | collect some wood.
12. The policeman | is telling him | to | stop.
    The policeman | is telling him | not to | stop.
13. There are | as many | people here | as | over there.
    There are not | so many | tins of food | in Picture A | as | in Picture B.
14. The two hunters are running away so quickly | that | they drop their gun.
15. Can you please | tell me | how to | go to the Post Office?
    Can you please | direct me | to | the police station?
16. Before | putting the tube into water, | pump it up.
    Mark the spot | before | sticking the patch on.
17. Although | a boy is trying to catch the ball, | he cannot reach it.
18. While | the old man is sleeping | the monkeys take the hats.
    The monkeys take the hats | while | the old man is sleeping
19. The gardener | must | sweep up all the leaves.
20. They do not | notice | a storm beginning.
    Dick is | ready to | dive into the sea.
21. The boy is asking | the rich man | if | he can study in the big house.
    The boy is asking | the rich man | to | let him study in the big house.
22. The children do not know | what | to do.
23. The road is | too | narrow | for | the car to pass.
24. It is | possible | to | weigh the baskets of stones.
25. David and Ann ate the food | that | Mrs Brown made.
26. The merchant pleased no one | because | he tried to please everyone.
27. He was so far in front | that | he took a rest.
28. The blind man thought | that | the rich woman had given him the money.
29. The two boys ran to the river | so as to | look for their ball.
    The two boys ran to the river | so that | they could look for their ball.
30. The thief turned | on | the small radio.
    The thief turned | the small radio | on.
31. He hit the tiger | as hard as | he could.
    The innkeeper tried to | stop him | going.
32. The boy | whom | he left | put out the fire.
    The boy | whose | books were burning | put out the fire.

2 Helpful Phrases
for describing pictures

in the foreground
in the background
in the distance
in the middle-distance
in the middle
at | in the centre
on the horizon
in sight
out of sight
on the left
on the right
on the left-hand side
on the right-hand side
in the top left-hand corner
in the top right-hand corner
in the bottom left-hand corner
in the bottom right-hand corner
at the top (of the picture)
at the bottom (of the picture)